D0398027

50 OF THE FINEST

After Dinner Games

LAGOON
BOOKS

Series Editor: Heather Dickson
Editor and Games compiler: Sylvia Goulding
Design: Rosamund Saunders
Illustrator: Gaby Wirminghaus
Additional contributors: Ann Marangos and Sheila Harding
Cover design: Gary Inwood Studios

Published by:
LAGOON BOOKS
PO BOX 311, KT2 5QW, UK
www.lagoongames.com

ISBN: 1902813057

50 OF THE FINEST

After Dinner Games

Introduction

This book, with its fun collection of party games, is the perfect accompaniment for any dinner party or late-night gathering. Compiled by an eclectic group of games enthusiasts, it contains, not only a game for any occasion, but a game for everyone …

If you've over-indulged and can't get up from the table, then why not try…

Snip Snap Snorem, Tip-Tap-Top, Your Round, My Next Lover or *Bleep.*

But if it's something more rowdy that you're after which involves a bit more action, then look up …

Coin Curling, Citrus Bowls, Beat the Intro, Nimble Thimble, Dr Doolittle and *Quack Quack.*

If it's something fun, which Great Auntie Edna might also enjoy, then try …

Ninety-Nine, Book Prize, Kim's Box, In Tune, Guess What? or *I, Calculus.*

But if it's something a bit saucier that you're after, look up …

Stripping Suits, Bottled Knee, How do you like it? and *Reservoir Snogs.*

If you're wanting to show off your intellect, then try …
    Span the Bridge, *Taboo or not Taboo*, *Where in the World?*, *Foreign Creatures* or *Stickety Wickety*.

But if you're only good at knocking back the beer, then look up …
    Left-Right, *Drink a Tower* or *Inebriated Newts*.

Whatever you choose, 50 of the Finest After Dinner Games is the perfect way to round off your evening in style!

RULES

Each game has been clearly described and where items are required in order to play any of the games they have been listed under the title of each game.

FORFEITS

Many of the games require forfeits to be paid. To help players decide on something suitably spiteful to dish out to their fellow guests, we've provided a few suggestions on pp. 18, 42, 60 and 92.

WARNING

Some of the games in this book involve drinking. If played with alcoholic beverages, we urge you to exercise moderation in consumption!

Contents

Fade to Grey

YOU WILL NEED:
SIX OR MORE PLAYERS

A fast and furious memory game, which is made all the more confusing the more mistakes your guests make!

This game makes people change colour – no, they don't blush, but in their confusion they will slowly fade away and turn an ashen shade of grey!

Seat everyone around the table or in a circle on the floor. Now assign all players a colour: Blue, Red, Green, Pink, Yellow, Purple, and so on, not following any particular order, except that the last player is Grey. If you have a large number of guests, you may need to include more specific colours like burgundy, crimson and emerald, or even pastel pink or apple-blossom white! Check that everyone knows their own as well as everybody else's colour.

Now start a rhythm by slapping the table and clapping your hands, like this: table – table – clap – table – table – clap. Once all have the rhythm, say "Blue" (your own colour) – table – table – "to Red" (another player's colour) – clap. Without missing a beat, Red has to pass play to another player.

Continue until someone fluffs it. As soon as one player misses a beat, or gets their own or the next person's colour wrong, they "fade to Grey". This means, they swap places – and colours – with the person to their left, moving in the direction of Grey. Now the game continues, with two people having taken on new identities. As more and more mistakes happen, and people swap identities at the rate of knots, it'll get ever harder to stop yourself from laughing. Perhaps this is the time to start introducing forfeits…

FOR FORFEIT IDEAS SEE PAGES 18, 42, 60 AND 92

8

Guys and Dolls

YOU WILL NEED:
TWO OR MORE PLAYERS, MALE AND FEMALE
PAPER AND PENS
CATEGORY CARDS, PREPARED IN ADVANCE

Find out who's really wearing the trousers, the men or the women, in this fun team game!

Prepare the category cards in advance. On each card, write a subject and then ten examples. Make the subjects specific to men and women and mark them on the back of the card (D for dolls, and G for guys). See the next page for a list of subject ideas.

Divide into teams, with all men in one, all women in the other team. Each team has to pick a card for the opposite team, and read out their subject. Now teams have to race each other, trying to think of as many examples that might be on the category card as they can. The first team to finish shouts "Stop", and all answers are read out.

SCORING: score 1 point if the answers are listed on the card, and 2 points if they are not listed but accepted by the opposite team.

Here are some examples of subjects:

GUYS: 10 brands of beers; 10 science fiction writers; 10 heavy rock bands; 10 brands of aftershave; 10 "large" women; 10 parts of a car engine; 10 things men find easier than women; 10 electric power tools; 10 terms of endearment men use for their girlfriends or wives; 10 things that men do on most days.

DOLLS: 10 things women find irritating in men; 10 perfume brands; 10 ways for a woman to flirt with a man; 10 famous TV chefs; 10 foreign-language expressions that are used in English; 10 popular garden flowers; 10 ways of saving money; 10 Mediterranean islands.

You get the idea…

Ninety-Nine

YOU WILL NEED:
TWO TO FOUR PLAYERS
1 PACK OF CARDS
PAPER AND PEN

In this card race you are trying to be
the *last* past the post, that is you
are trying *not* to reach a score of
Ninety-Nine. Trick cards may
help – or hinder!

Cut for deal, then deal each player
four cards. Place the remaining pack
face down on the table. All picture
cards and the Ace count 10,
all other cards their face
value – except for the trick cards!
The player to the dealer's left places one of their
cards face up on the table. This is the start of the
"Ninety-Nine" pack, and you will need to keep a
running total. They must pick a new card from the
face-down pile, and play passes to the left.

The second player now places one of their cards on top and announces the new total.

The trick cards are the key to winning and should be treasured by the player who picks them up. They can be used to pass or reverse play, and to subtract from the total – so keep them and hold them back until you can use them to your own advantage—and the disadvantage of other players!

King = automatically brings the total to 99;
   4 = reverses direction of play;
   9 = a "pass" card: nothing is added to the total and play just passes to the next person;
 10 = subtracts 10 from the score.

WINNING: If a player cannot play a card without raising the total beyond 99, they are out of the game. The winner is the last person to stay in the game.

Problem Solving

YOU WILL NEED:
ANY NUMBER OF PLAYERS,
APT AT SOLVING PROBLEMS AND
MANAGING CRISIS SITUATIONS

This is a game of misunderstandings – the questions will bear no – or only little – relation to the answers!

Ask one player to leave the room. While they are outside, decide on a crisis. This should be a serious, embarrassing or possibly life-changing problem, for example, accidentally running over the neighbour's pet rabbit, watching a large bank note drop out of another person's pocket, or surprising your spouse in bed with your best friend.

Ask the player back in. They will now have to ask everyone in turn what they would do in a particular situation, changing the scenario from player to player. The other

players will all answer truthfully. However, they will not answer the questions they have just been asked, but will instead say what they would do if they were in the crisis everyone had chosen in the questioner's absence. And the questioner needs to find out what crisis had been chosen.

The dialogue might sound something like this:

PRE-DECIDED CRISIS: You were drunk at the office party and fell asleep under the boss' desk. It is morning, and the boss has just come into the office.

"What would you do if Kim Basinger sat next to you at the movies?" – "Apologize profusely and leave as fast as possible."

"What would you do if the police found you naked tied to a lamppost after a stag party?" – "Quickly present three ideas for making company savings."

"What would you do if you broke your mother-in-law's favourite ornament?" – "Say, 'I've been waiting for you, come into my arms darling.'"

Quick on the Draw

YOU WILL NEED:
TWO PLAYERS OR MORE
A PILLOW CASE
ASSORTED OBJECTS
BLINDFOLD
PAPER AND PEN

Not a shooting game, as you might think, but a game for partners. It will prove a whole number of things – how well  you can describe something, how well you can draw it, and even how well can you relate to each other.

In advance, assemble a number of objects in a pillowcase. Include, for example, a banana, a video cassette, a notepad, a pair of earings and an alarm clock. Get people to pair up, either with their own partner or by drawing names out of a hat. One couple plays at a time.

Get one person to blindfold the other one, and give paper and pen to the blindfolded person. Now the other person takes an object out of the pillow case,

 and starts to describe it to their partner. They are not allowed to say what it is, or explain the object in words. Instead, they have to describe it as a geometric object. For example, a banana should not be described as a fruit, but as a longish, curved, almost round cylinder shape, with slightly tapered ends. Similarly, the alarm clock becomes a round object with attachments, engineered to emit signals, or something like that. You should also help the "artist" by directing their pen, "up a bit, left a bit, that's it, draw a line, upwards, a bit longer".

At the end all the drawings are compared to the actual objects and will be judged by other guests. They should be awarded realism and recognizability points. If, however, you have a real Picasso or Dali in your midst, it might be a good idea to set a special award aside to honour their talents!

Tip-Tap-Top

YOU WILL NEED:
ANY NUMBER OF GUESTS
A COIN PER PLAYER

Concentration is all that is needed to succeed here – but who can boast of that, especially after a long evening?

Each player holds a coin in their hand. The first person taps it on the table once while saying "tip" and play moves to the left; twice while saying "tap, tap" and play moves to the right; three times while saying "top, top, top" and play moves to the person sitting opposite the speaker.

All this should happen at great speed. When someone gets it wrong and taps out of turn, says the wrong words, or says them the wrong number of times, they have to pay a forfeit or have a drink.

FOR
FORFEIT
IDEAS
SEE PAGES
18, 42, 60
AND 92

Forfeits

DRAW NUMBERS, OR JUST USE THEM ONE AFTER THE OTHER.

1. Compose and sing a song about earthworms, to the tune of "Twinkle, twinkle, little star".

2. Kiss the most attractive person in the room.

3. Exchange 2 items of clothing with someone of the opposite sex.

4. Name three ex-lovers.

5. Give an agreed sum of money to a stranger NOW.

6. Confess your greatest sin.

7. Collect, within three minutes, 1 bottle, 1 glass of water, 1 sweet, 1 matchstick, 1 bra, and 1 sock which is not your own.

8. Answer "yes" or "no" to 3 questions before you hear them: Do you drink like a fish? eat like a pig? laugh like a horse?

9. Touch the 4 corners of the room within 15 seconds.

10. Parrot everything that is being said during the next round.

After Dinner Lotto

YOU WILL NEED:
FOUR GUESTS OR MORE
PIECES OF PAPER WITH NUMBERS FROM 1-30
LOTTERY SLIPS

The odds are good in this game, but beware, life's a lottery and, as happens so often in life, good luck and fortune are not always what they seem…

FOR FORFEIT IDEAS SEE PAGES 18, 42, 60 AND 92

Prepare little pieces of paper with numbers from, say, 1 to 30. Now ask everyone to fill in a lottery slip, ticking six numbers each, also between 1 and 30. Ask all the guests to make sure that their name is written on the lottery slip so that they will be able to claim their prize later in the evening.

After a short interlude, draw six numbers and announce these. Everyone will get very excited and compare them with their own lottery slips, but now comes the surprise: instead of fantastic fortunes, your guests will win forfeits! If they have all six numbers that were drawn, they'll have to perform six forfeits, if they have no correct numbers then they're all right – they get off scot-free!

Span the Bridge

YOU WILL NEED:
ABOUT 4-8 PLAYERS WHO
ENJOY WORD GAMES
PAPER AND PEN FOR EACH PERSON

A mental race against the clock – who will come up with the longest words to bridge the gap between two other words?

To start with, each player has to think of a six-letter word. They should write this word vertically down the left-hand side of their piece of paper, then repeat the same word up the right-hand side of the paper, so it reads backwards. Now they should pass the paper to their neighbour.

The race starts now.

Each player has to try and think of words that "span the bridge", starting and ending with the given letters. Every new word needs to have at least four letters, and each bridging letter counts as a point. If, for example, your chosen word was *carpet*, then the grid could look like this:

C A U G H **T** = 4 points

A R A B L **E** = 4 points

R E A **P** = 2 points

P O O **R** = 2 points

E M M **A** = 2 points

T E R R I F I **C** = 6 points

making a total of 20 points.

If your guests are very wordly wise, you could add a few rules of your own to this game, to make it a little more difficult. For example, you could decide not to allow any names, or indeed, to use only the names of famous film stars. You could also give extra points for some hard-to-place letters such as Q, V, X, Y and Z, or you could agree to give special bonus points for every rude word…

Your Round

At the end of this game you'll wish you had fewer friends … or a better memory!

Imagine you're sitting in a pub and it's your turn to buy everyone a drink. Ever been in that sort of situation? Isn't it infuriating that everyone places a different order? And that some people even change their mind half-way through ordering? That's what this game is all about.

The first person picks two of the other guests, for example, Heather and Jim, and says: "Heather went to the bar and ordered one rum and coke for Jim." One after another, everyone around the table repeats this, until the last person finishes with the same phrase "Heather went to the bar and ordered one rum and coke for Jim and said 'keep the change'."

For the next round, another person and a different drink are added, the more complicated, the better. For example: "Heather went to the bar and ordered one rum and coke for Jim, and two tequila slammers with salt around the rim for Ros and Gaby." Again everyone else has to repeat the order.

And so it goes on … and on … until the first person fluffs their order. They'll have to pay a forfeit (or buy the next round…).

Some ideas for orders at the bar: *a campari and soda, a packet of salsa-flavoured crisps, two vodka and orange, three port and lemon, one bourbon and coke, one glass of lemonade with ice, two glasses of medium-dry white wine…*

FOR FORFEIT IDEAS SEE PAGES 18, 42, 60 AND 92

Citrus Bowls

YOU WILL NEED:
TWO TO EIGHT PLAYERS
2 ORANGES AND 1 LEMON PER PLAYER
DICE

A fruity version of bowls, that can be played equally well indoors on the carpet in winter, or outdoors in the summer.

Make sure that there is quite a bit of space for this game. If there are more than two players, divide guests into two teams. Throw the dice for the highest number to see who will go first. Every player should mark the peel of their oranges and lemons with their initial or any other symbol, so they can be recognized later. (One orange looks very much like another, after all.)

The first player rolls the dice across the floor, then takes their first orange and attempts to roll it so it will end up as close to the dice as possible. Now the other players take it in turn to do the same with their own fruit – while, of course, also trying to knock everyone else's oranges out of the way.

In the last round, everyone has to roll a lemon – this fruit will of course follow a less predictable route across the carpet!

The player whose citrus fruit all end up closest to the dice wins. You could award points as follows: 1 point per orange, 2 points per lemon, that are closest to the dice; and the winner of the first round could have to play with a "handicap" in the next: rolling two lemons and one orange, for example.

This game can be fairly exhausting – make sure you have lots of refreshments ready for afterwards … orange juice, lemon juice … or, perhaps more to your guests' liking, some delicious cocktails with oranges and lemons!

Quick-Fire

Establish a good, fast rhythm, and this quick-fire word game should give cause for many a forfeit to be played!

Players should sit in a circle. Start a regular rhythm by getting everyone to click their fingers. Now Player One says a word, and Player Two has to follow with a new word that either rhymes with the first one or starts with the same initial. The new word has to be said before the fourth click. Player Three has to continue with another rhyming or alliterating word, again before the fourth click.

It could go like this, for example: "dirty" – click – click – click – "door" – click – click – click – "more" – click – click – click – "pinafore" – click – click – click – "please" and so on … until someone gets it wrong.

The constant clicking rhythm is almost hypnotic and quite brain-numbing – you'll be amazed how hard it is to think of a suitable word when it's your turn! Very soon, spurred along by the relentless rhythm, people will start making up non-existent rhyming words, or they'll just look completely blank. But … every mistake has to be paid for with a forfeit.

FOR FORFEIT IDEAS SEE PAGES 18, 42, 6O AND 92

As the game progresses, you could speed up the clicking rhythm, or make everyone answer before the third click.

Alternatively, you could introduce more rules, say every word beginning in "S" reverses the direction of play, and every word beginning in "B" has to be followed by taking off an item of clothing, whether the word was rhyming or not…

Coin Curling

YOU WILL NEED:
FOUR OR SIX PLAYERS
PAPER, MARKER PEN
4 COINS PER PLAYER

Forget the Winter Olympics! The kitchen table is where the real battles are being fought!

First mark out your target on a large piece of paper. Draw three concentric circles, as shown below. (You could copy these circles if you have some greaseproof paper.) Mark a starting point, in line with the dotted line, at a distance of about 18in/50cm from the target.

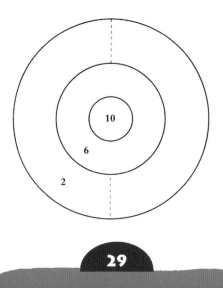

The game is played as a series of knock-out contests, with two players competing at a time. Agree the number of rounds each couple play. The first couple starts, with the first player flipping two of their coins from the starting point towards the target. The second player now flips their two coins, again aiming towards the target, but at the same time trying to dislodge any high-scoring coins of their opponent's. Both players complete the round with their other two coins.

SCORING. If you manage to flick your coin so it finishes exactly on the target, you score the number of points shown. If your coin ends up lying on one of the lines, you score the higher value. Only coins that still score after both players have flipped all their coins, count as points.

Taboo or not Taboo?

This is an after-dinner version of the old favourite "Taboo", with some additional complications.

Divide into two teams. Each team has to write down 20 objects, each word on a separate sheet of paper. Underline these main words.

Now write three words underneath that are obviously connected with the main word – these are to be the taboo words. For example, if your chosen word is *banana,* then you could make your taboo words *fruit, yellow* and *tropical.*

Finally, write down two non-taboo words which should be *not at all* connected with the main word. You could choose, for example, *red* and *bus.*

Now the fun starts. Papers should be turned over and swapped with the other team. The first person draws a sheet of paper and, without showing it to other members of their team, starts to describe the object. In the description, however, they are not allowed to use the taboo words, but *must* use the non-taboo words. A connection between the object and the non-taboo words has to be established, but it is not permissible to just assert "it's not a fire extinguisher", for example, if the non-taboo word is "fire extinguisher".

The other team members have exactly one minute to try their luck and guess what object is being described. If they do find the answer, they collect a point, and the next person in their team starts with a new sheet. If, however, within this minute they aren't able to guess what the object is, play passes to the other team.

Identity Crisis

YOU WILL NEED:
SIX PLAYERS OR MORE
HEADBANDS OR RIBBONS FOR EVERY PLAYER
IDENTITY CARDS, ABOUT THE SIZE OF A PLAYING
CARD, PREPARED IN ADVANCE
PEN

The object of this game is to find out who you are. Everyone else knows, but you are left in the dark and have to guess.

Prepare some identity cards in advance – write the name of a famous person on each one. Ask each guest to tie a headband or ribbon around their head and to pick an identity card, making sure they do not read the name on it. They should now stick the card behind their headband so that all the other players can read it.

Now everyone has to start guessing at their own identity by asking questions of the other players around the table. One person starts, and asks a question beginning with "Am I …" of everyone else. They could ask, for example, "Am I dead? Am I fat? Am I a singer? Am I a bore?" Once their question has been answered, the next player is allowed to ask one question of everyone else. The first player to guess their identity correctly wins.

You could theme your identities depending on the real and mental age of your guests – and their level of alcohol consumption! Choose, for example, only names from TV or Greek philosophers. You could also make the game even more difficult by including objects, such as favourite desserts, or even abstract ideas and theories.

Here are some ideas for identities: *Ruby Wax; Jerry Springer; the entire cast of Friends; Aristotle; Brad Pitt; Mohammed; Genghis Khan; Paul Newman; Hillary Clinton; the Spice Girls; the Ugly Duckling; the Wizard of Oz; Pavarotti; Maggie Thatcher; the Tower of London; Lake Ontario; a floppy disk; the Millennium bug; the border between France and Spain; the riddle of the Sphinx; the theory of relativity; eternal happiness.*

Left-Right

This game may seem to have military overtones, yet you'll end up – not with regimental discipline – but total chaos!

Have everyone sit around the table, with their full glasses (or bottles…) in front of them.

Now get some discipline into the group and shout: "Left (pause); Left (pause); Left – Right – Left." In rhythm, all players have to pass their glasses to the person next to them, left or right, depending on which command has been shouted. So each glass has to be passed three times to the left, then to the right, and finally to the left again. It may take a little practice.

Everyone who gets it wrong – and, as we all know, the more advanced the evening the more likely this is to happen! – has to either finish the drink in front of them (hopefully it won't be a Crème de Menthe!), or perform a forfeit.

Once all your guests have got the hang of this game (which might take a little while), you could try to carry on silently – the order of play always stays the same: Left – Left – Left-Right-Left.

For another variation, you could try singing a marching or walking tune while passing the glasses around, such as "I love to go a-wandering", or, even better, a song that has a completely different rhythm. Try "Brown girl in the ring" or "YMCA" for a laugh. Chaos is bound to ensue rather rapidly.

FOR FORFEIT IDEAS SEE PAGES 18, 42, 60 AND 92

Heads or Tails

YOU WILL NEED:
AN AUDIENCE
6 LARGE COINS
BLINDFOLD

A magic trick to stun your audience – and perhaps surprise yourself as well!

Ask your audience to arrange the six coins in a circle on the table, with any combination of heads or tails showing. Without making it obvious, count and memorize the number of tails that are showing. Now ask to be blindfolded. Leave the room, and say you wish to avoid hearing the coins being turned over. Ask your audience to turn over as many coins as they wish, as long as they always turn two at a time.

As soon as they feel they're done, return and ask the others to place your hand on a coin of their choice. Then take off your blindfold, and tell them accurately, whether the concealed coin has heads or tails showing.

The way you do this is by remembering whether it was an odd or an even number of tails showing when you left the room. Once your blindfold has come off, quickly check whether the visible coins show an odd or an even number of tails. If both answers are the same, then the covered coin is heads; if they are different, then it is tails.

Your audience may think you only guessed, having a 50:50 chance of getting it right. You should therefore convince them that you really *do* know, by repeating the trick as many times as they wish!

Where in the World?

YOU WILL NEED:
TWO OR MORE PLAYERS
PAPER AND PENS

An after-dinner test of people's knowledge of cities and countries? That's only the starting point. It gets more involved as you carry on...

You could play in teams, or make it a free-for-all. In the first round, each player (or each team) has to think of a location. This could be a country or a town, a river or a mountain, but also a specific building, for example the Empire State Building.

The first player asks "Where in the World am I?". All the others (or the other team) have to find out by asking questions to which the first player has to reply with "yes" or "no". Once everyone has guessed where you are, move on to the second round.

Round 2: now everyone has to think of a famous personality linked with that location – whether alive or dead, real or imagined – and the question is "Who in the World am I with?"

Round 3: come up with an activity that you and the chosen person could be doing together. Question: "What in the World am I doing?"

Round 4: think of a way in which you are doing it. Question: "How in the World am I doing it?"

The guessers collect a point every time their question is answered with a "yes", and five points if they find one of the four answers. They lose a point every time the answer is "no". The person with the most points wins. Some examples: *screamingly roller-coasting with Mickey Mouse in Disneyland; tenderly bathing with Cleopatra in Alexandria; passionately snogging Leo DiCaprio on the Titanic.*

Feather Race

YOU WILL NEED:
A LARGE GROUP OF PEOPLE
2 OR MORE DOWNY FEATHERS
2 PAPER PLATES

A feather-light-hearted relay race, for which you will need a lot of space – it is probably best played outdoors in summer, unless there is a strong breeze blowing.

Divide everyone into two teams, and mark lines at opposite ends of the room or garden. When the starting signal is given, the first player in each team has to put a feather on their plate, take the plate in their mouth, "race" to the finish line and back to their team. There they pass the plate, from mouth to mouth, to the next player, who will "race" off immediately. If the feather blows away, the player has to return to the start line and start again.

The winner is the first team where each player has carried the feather to the finish line and back.

Forfeits

TEN MORE IDEAS FOR FORFEITS

1. Walk twice around the room, wearing the shoes of the person to your left.

2. Stand on the table as still as a statue for 5 minutes.

3. Make up a ten-line poem about the most attractive person in the room.

4. Tell everyone how you lost your virginity.

5. Whistle "I'm dreaming of a white Christmas."

6. Choose before you hear the alternatives: Should the person on your right (a) slap your cheeks, (b) kiss you, or (c) stamp on your toes?

7. Walk across the room on hands and feet (not knees), holding a tin in each hand.

8. Whisper a secret into the ear of the person to your left.

9. Kiss the least attractive person in the room.

10. Allow everyone in the room to tickle you, without laughing.

My Next Lover

This is really more of a puzzle than a game, but it should cause some hilarity, and keep your friends guessing for a while.

Start the game by describing one person in the room as your next lover, for example "my next lover has blond hair". The other players have to guess who you are referring to. Instead of giving your lover's name, though, they have to add to the description, for example "my next lover wears a blue shirt".

What your guests will not realize straightaway is that you were not describing one particular person, but using a code. "My next lover" could mean, for example, "the person to my right", or "the nearest person of the opposite sex", or "the nearest person to the left with

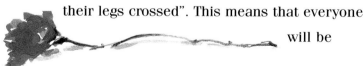

their legs crossed". This means that everyone will be

describing a different person, making it very difficult for the guessing crowd to fathom what's going on.

The first speaker has to tell the second speaker whether their description is correct or not. Then the third person continues. Once a player has "got it", they should just carry on playing, obviously now making accurate statements.

When there is only one player left who still doesn't have a clue about who is being described, please put them out of their misery! Explain the code. And while you're at it, why not impose some hefty forfeits?

FOR
FORFEIT
IDEAS
SEE PAGES
18, 42, 60
AND 92

Unconnected

YOU WILL NEED:
ANY NUMBER OF PLAYERS
A LATERAL- AND FAST-THINKING BRAIN,
FULL OF NONSENSE

To play this game, it helps if you are slightly – or even extremely – mad!

It's easy to find words that have something to do with each other, but here the challenge is the exact opposite: to find a series of words that have absolutely no connection!

The first player has an easy time – they can just say anything that comes into their mind. The next player, however, has to find a word that is absolutely and definitely unconnected with this first word. The first word could be, for example, "dentist", and this could then be followed by "rain", and "rain" by "red" – words that, under normal circumstances, are never associated with each other at all.

And then the fun starts, because all the other players have to try and challenge players' words. So, you may proudly suggest that "paper" has nothing to do with "lettuce", but immediately comes the cry "lettuce can be wrapped in paper" – and unfortunately you have lost!

The challenges will get ever more spurious, but, of course, the challengers may also lose points, if they cannot prove a reasonable and generally agreed connection between the two words. In the case of "dentist" and "rain", for example, one player might suggest that he always visits the dentist when it rains. This should be discounted…

It certainly helps, if you've had a couple of drinks, and if your head is generally full of weird, wicked, and wonderful ideas. The appointment of an adjudicator to settle disputes might also be a good idea.

Book Prize

YOU WILL NEED:
EIGHT GUESTS OR MORE
PEN AND PAPER FOR EACH PLAYER
WORD CARDS, PREPARED IN ADVANCE

Play this game when the mood is not too rowdy, and guests wish to play something a little more refined and generally quieter. There's ample scope for people with a vivid imagination to make everyone laugh…or bore all the other guests to tears! Prepare some word cards in advance, at least six per person. Choose words that have little or nothing to do with each other, including some abstract words and some concrete words, some that describe an activity and some that describe a property. Long words usually work out particularly well. Pick some rude words, too, for extra fun.

When you are ready to play, give every guest pen and paper, and make them draw about six word cards each. Set the clock to an agreed time, say five minutes. Now everyone has to incorporate the words they picked into a reasonably coherent story, using each word at least once.

When the time is over, each player has to read their story out loud. When everyone has finished, you can vote on originality and style, giving points out of ten for each story, and awarding the coveted book prize to the best one.

Here are some examples for words you could put on the word cards: *glove; depression; dancing; cantankerous; anatomically; torture; underwear; shoe factory; dichotomy; breasts; exasperated; waterfall; protuberance; breathing apparatus; lovemaking; weather forecast; itching; marketing expertise; tickled pink; rhinoceros; holiday resort; chocolate pudding; wicked; scarlet; silicone; muddy...*

Kim's Box

YOU WILL NEED:
SIX PLAYERS OR MORE
A BOX WITH ASSORTED OBJECTS
A TIMER
PAPER AND PENS

This is a combination of the well-known "Kim's Game", beloved by children, and the mythical Greek Pandora's Box – out of which all sorts of evil will emerge!

Prepare a cardboard box or a tray with 20–30 assorted objects, the stranger the better. (For ideas of objects to include see over the page.)

Reveal the box, and allow all guests to study its contents for two full minutes. Now cover it up, and give players a set period of time, say five minutes, to write down everything they remember. And make sure they do not cheat and compare their results!

Once everyone's finished, check their answers, and note the objects they have forgotten. Also assign the names of two people who are present to each player. Now everyone has five minutes to write a story about those two guests, involving all the objects from the box that they had forgotten to list.

At the end, all the stories will be read out and judged for originality, with extra points for making everyone laugh.

Some ideas for objects to include in the box: *a steaming cup of coffee; dog biscuit; laddered tights; paperback romance; Y-fronts; drinking straw; cucumber; tennis ball; razor blades; KY jelly; floppy disk; post-it note with writing; pin-up picture; a sticky plaster; a chocolate chip cookie; half a dozen paperclips; a Russian dictionary; a handful of nails; a single glove; false eyelash; fork; fuse; a polkadot bikini; pen knife; light bulb; a pen; tin opener; a chocolate wrapper; a plastic carnation.*

Nimble Thimble

YOU WILL NEED:
EIGHT PLAYERS OR MORE
A STRAW FOR EACH PLAYER
TWO THIMBLES

Less haste, more speed could be the motto of this race for the nimble-mouthed.

Divide everyone into two teams. If you have an uneven number of guests, one person could be chosen to act as the referee.

Now equip every player with a straw, and give a thimble to the person in each team who has been chosen to start the race.

(Thimbles are a dying breed, of course, but if you really cannot beg, steal, or borrow two, just use two paper cups instead.)

When the whistle is blown (or other start signal given), the two teams have to race each other by passing the thimble from person to person, until they reach the end of the team line. If this sounds easy, think again, for the thimble has to be balanced on the end of a straw which is held in the mouth. The next player has to pick up the thimble with their straw, also held in their mouth. And hands are definitely not allowed! You will find this is more difficult than it sounds, and will lead to all sorts of contortions as players try to prevent the thimble from dropping off the end of their straws.

If the thimble – or one of the straws – is dropped, the thimble has to go back to the first player for a fresh start. This is where a referee comes in handy…

All team members are free to egg on their own players with loud shouting and other forms of encouragement. The more noise this creates, the better for the overall level of enjoyment.

And if you wish to make things more difficult for the other team, the best you can do is laugh uncontrollably when one of their players experiences difficulties. Laughter is catching, and balancing a thimble on a straw becomes almost impossible for a player once they start laughing too!

A Vowel, Please

YOU WILL NEED:
TWO OR MORE PLAYERS
LETTER SQUARES, FROM SCRABBLE GAME
OR HAND-WRITTEN
TWO BOXES OR BAGS
A TIMER

Test your word power – against the other players or team – in a race against time!

This game can be played by individual players or in teams. You will need the letters from a Scrabble game or make up your own. If you write your own, make sure there is more than one E, A, I, S, R, N and T as well as any other common letters. Separate the letters into vowels and consonants and place them in two boxes or bags.

This may be a good moment to provide everyone with a cup of hot coffee, to liven up sleepy intellects and alert bleary eyes, before the challenges of the game overwhelm your guests.

Now each player (or team) asks for eight letters, choosing consonants or vowels as they see fit. The letters are revealed for all to see. The clock is set to one minute, and every player (or team) has to try and come up with the longest possible word, using as many of the given letters as they can.

Every letter counts one point, and the person/team with the most points wins.

Alternatively, ask people or teams to come up with as many *different* words of three letters or more from their letters. Give them a little more time for this, say three or five minutes. Then count each letter in a word as 1 point, and each word as two points. Give bonus points for "difficult" letters such as Q, Z and X.

If your guests are very wordly-wise, you can always introduce extra complications by demanding that all words relate to a particular subject like features of the countryside, or words relating to the weather, or that they should only be proper nouns.

In the case of disputed words, consult a dictionary or argue until you can agree or get bored with disagreeing! Then play another game…

Bleep

YOU WILL NEED:
ANY NUMBER OF PLAYERS
A BLEEPER (BELL, SAUCEPAN LID
AND SPOON, OR SIMILAR)

T his is a great – and potentially very noisy – game
of verbal trickery.

First choose a referee who decides on a word that
is taboo. This should be a frequently used word, for
example "and", "I", "the" or similar. Now you can
either have everyone question one victim, or one
person questioning everyone else.
Whichever rule you follow, the
person who is interrogated
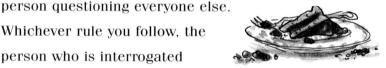
needs to answer very quickly, without hesitation, and
without using the taboo word(s).

The questioners fire questions at the hapless
victim(s), fast and furiously: "What did you do
yesterday? Who else went there? You asked whom?"
and so on, always trying to entice the interrogee to
answer with the banned words, "*I* went there", "John

and Mary went with me", and so on. If they use any of the taboo words accidentally, the referee will bleep them loudly, ring the bell or bang the saucepan lid, just so that everyone knows – they're out.

Make this game even more difficult by declaring a letter taboo in addition to the word, for example the letter "L". Now this letter is not permitted in any word in the answers either, and the interrogee has to substitute non-L words, for example using "ascend" instead of "climb". (It's best not to choose a vowel, though, because these occur too frequently.) Give a ten-second time limit for every answer to a question, because people will quickly get bored if everyone spends hours trying to think of a clever answer.

You can combine this game with the old favourite "Sixty Seconds", or "Just a Minute". Give each person a subject they have to speak about for one minute, all the while not using the taboo word and/or letter, and make sure they speak for a full minute without repeating themselves or hesitating. The successful speaker should be rewarded with a drink (or another helping of chocolate pudding!).

Stripping Suits

YOU WILL NEED:
THREE TO SIX PLAYERS
1 PACK OF PLAYING CARDS

There is a real incentive for trying to win this card game – for each time you lay down a suit, you get to ask your fellow players to take off an article of clothing!

Deal out all the cards to the players. Now the player to the dealer's left starts by asking any other player for a specific card, say 8♦. To do this, they must hold a card of the same value, say an 8♥. Players, who hold the card they have been asked for, have to hand it over, and the first player is allowed another go. Player One may continue for as long as they are successful. Play passes to their left if they have asked a person for a card they do not hold.

As soon as one player has all four cards of the same value, they shout "suit", and lay the cards out on the table. And this is the exciting bit for each time a complete suit is laid down, the successful player can ask all the others to take off an item of clothing, according to the value of the cards in their suit:

1 = left shoe

2 = right shoe

3 = socks

4 = men only: tie

5 = jumpers/sweatshirts

6 = men only: trousers

7 = women only: dress/skirt/trousers

8 = shirt/blouse

9 = jewellery/watch

10 = women only: tights/stockings/suspenders

Jack = strip to waist

Queen = women only: bra

King = men only: underpants

Ace = you're allowed to put one item back on…

Guess What?

You need a fair amount of imagination for this game – the idea is to act or portray an object by miming it to other guests.

Write out the object cards in advance, adjusting the degree of difficulty (or rudeness) to suit your invited guests.

One player takes an object card, then has to mime the object written on it. Pointing is not allowed, neither is talking. But the person miming is allowed to nod encouragingly or shake their head. Everyone else has to guess, and every correct guess wins a point. Ideas for object cards:

curtain; bra; apple; condom; coffee cup; tree; nipple; candle; a shoe; a champagne cork; computer mouse; underpants; pencil … and so on.

Forfeits

1. Answer "yes" or "no" to three questions before you hear them. Question 1: "Are you good looking?" Question 2: "Are you rich?" Question 3: "Are you good in bed?"

2. Find your partner while blindfolded, by touching and feeling everyone in the room.

3. Kiss the person on your right on the mouth for at least 10 seconds, but no longer than 20 seconds.

4. Compose a song about trout, to the melody of "The hills are alive with the sound of music".

5. Eat a plate of "left-overs" from the dinner table.

6. Eat a water biscuit, then whistle the National Anthem – without showering your neighbours with crumbs.

7. Kiss the feet of everyone who's playing.

8. Confess your wildest fantasy.

9. Drink a pint of water down in one.

10. Finish the drink on your right.

I, Calculus

YOU WILL NEED:
A BALLOON
PENCIL AND PAPER
A PIN
POSSIBLY A CALCULATOR

This is a magic trick, rather than a game, but it's fun to play on people and may even lead your guests to believe you're some sort of mathematical mind-reader!

Tell your audience that you can look right through them and read their minds, that you can even work out what they are going to think before they have thought of thinking it!

Ask them to write down a three-digit number. They can choose any number, as long as it fulfils one small condition: the first digit must be greater than the last by at least 2. So, 401 and 765 are acceptable, 406 and 769 are not.

Stare at your guests, then close your eyes, massaging your temples and concentrating hard, while they are thinking and writing down their number – just as if you were trying to tune into their minds.

Without them seeing it, write down the number 1089 on a piece of paper, fold it up and slip it into a balloon. Inflate the balloon and tie it up.

Now ask your guests to do some maths: ask them to reverse their number and subtract this from the original number, for example: 401 − 104 = 297. They should now take the new number and add it to its mirror image: 297 + 792.

The answer is 1089, and it will always be 1089, as long as the first condition has been met. Allow one guest to pop the balloon – to find your correct answer, and then sit back and enjoy the praise as everyone tells you how clever you are!

Snip Snap Snorem

YOU WILL NEED:
THREE TO EIGHT PLAYERS
1 SET OF PLAYING CARDS

This card game is as silly as it sounds, but your guests will end up playing it at ferocious speeds – and the discussion as to what a "snorem" might be will continue for days!

Cut for deal, then deal out all cards. Players should sort their cards into suits, and sort each suit in a descending order, with Aces ranking low.

Now the player to the left of the dealer plays any card they wish, saying "Snip!" loud and clearly. If the card was, for example, the 8♥, then the player who holds the 7♥ plays it, saying "Snap!". This player is followed by whoever holds the 6♥, who says "Snorem!" while laying it on the table.

So far so good. Now, the

player with the 5♥ plays it, saying "Jig!", which stops the run. The "jigger" also starts a new sequence of cards, with any new card of their choice.

As the game continues, it will become ever more difficult, and eventually impossible, to complete sequences, because either the first card played is a 3 or lower, or because the following cards have already been played in previous runs. If this happens, the last card played is a "Stop" card. Stop cards behave much like "Jig" cards, allowing the stopper to start a new sequence.

Even "Snip" cards can become "Stop" cards – and thus help the player get rid of isolated cards in their hand with which they might otherwise be stuck until the end of the game.

It is important to judge carefully, which card should be played when – sometimes it is best to start a new sequence and hold some cards back till later, when they will come in handy.

The winner is the first player to get rid of all their cards – then have a drink, and start another game!

Dr Doolittle

YOU WILL NEED:
ANY NUMBER OF PLAYERS,
WITH A SENSE OF HUMOUR
A NUMBER OF SPEECH CARDS,
PREPARED IN ADVANCE

If you have an aptitude for learning foreign languages – or you simply yearn to moo like a cow or bark like a dog – then this is the game for you!

Set a time limit, for when you want to speak normally again – you'll probably find that people take to their roles so much that they'll just carry on and on, driving everyone bananas.

Now get everyone to draw a speech card. These cards tell you what your particular language is going to be, and for the set time limit each guest will have to speak as instructed by their card.

**FOR
FORFEIT
IDEAS
SEE PAGES
18, 42, 6O
AND 92**

If you make a mistake, you'll collect a forfeit point. (It may be a good idea, to secretly set up a tape recorder. Later in the evening, you  could play back to your guests what you recorded earlier – and set off a fresh wave of laughter.)

Here are some ideas for speech cards:

1. Moo like a cow after very use of the word 'and' (as in "Could I have another whisky and Moooo coke")

2. Bark like a mad dog – replace every "the" with a woof–woof (as in "Where is woof–woof toilet?)

3. Change all "S"s to "F"s (as in "thif if very filly")

4. Change all "I"s to "O"s (as in "thos os very solly")

5. Repeat the last syllable of every word with more than one syllable (as in "I wonder-der if Alison-son enjoys-joys her new apartment-ment")

6. Speak every proper noun backwards (as in "did you know that Eiram and Sicnarf have gone to Ecnarf?")

7. Insert a "boing" after every verb (as in "and then she said-boing that he should go-boing and sod-boing off".)

I Love my Love

YOU WILL NEED:
EIGHT PLAYERS OR MORE,
WITH A KNOWLEDGE OF THE ALPHABET

This is a ridiculously simple word game, but, played at speed, it may put you on the spot because the words just don't seem to come to mind...

Everyone sits in a circle. The first player starts by saying "I love my love because he/she is...", and then completes the phrase with an adjective and an adverb starting with "a", for example, "I love my love because she is amazingly ardent". The next player continues with "b", as in "bracingly brave", and so on.

You can make the game more boisterous by only allowing rude or nasty expressions such as "achingly awful" or "bloody big-headed". Or you could make it more difficult by starting with "z" and making everyone work their way backwards through the alphabet.

Roundtable Revenge

YOU WILL NEED:
EIGHT PLAYERS OR MORE

A game so silly, it beggars description! In fact, it'll be just as silly or rude as you and your guests are naturally!

Everyone sits around the table, and the loser of the previous game goes underneath the table. Now this daredevil can do whatever they like – tickle the back of somebody's knee, take their shoes off, tie two shoelaces together, or do other, even more unspeakable things.

Everyone around the table, meanwhile, has to keep a straight face and stare at their opposite number. If they start to laugh or giggle, they should have to pay a forfeit. But remember, don't be too harsh with the forfeits because the player who pays the forfeit gets to go under the table next to take their revenge...

Passionate Paperclips

YOU WILL NEED:
ANY NUMBER OF PLAYERS
A SMALL PIECE OF CARD (IDEALLY AN OLD
PLAYING CARD)
TWO LARGE PAPERCLIPS

This is really a magic trick rather than a game, but it never fails to amuse… Make sure you practise it a couple of times beforehand, to be sure you know what you're doing.

Get your guests into the right frame of mind. Tell them, that all paperclips are by nature wildly passionate, and, given half a chance, will go into a sizzling embrace as soon as you're not looking.

Now, in full view, attach the clips to the card, about 1in/2.5cm apart. Show both sides of the card to your guests to prove that everything is completely regular – nothing unusual.

Now fold the right-hand side of the card under the left clip. Turn the card around, and repeat, which should leave the card folded as a "Z" (see diagram overleaf). Straighten clips if necessary, especially if they have moved around the corner, then tug sharply at the ends of the card. The clips will shoot in the air – and to everyone's great amazement they will be joined in a passionate hug when they land (see diagram b).

DIAGRAM A

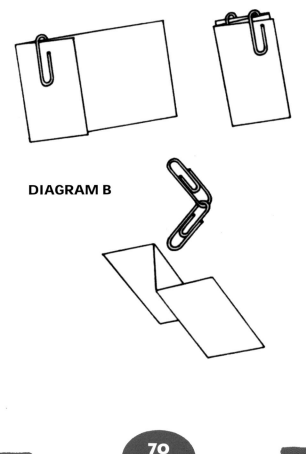

DIAGRAM B

Beat the Intro

YOU WILL NEED:
FOUR PLAYERS OR MORE
A DICE
SONG CARDS, PREPARED IN ADVANCE

Exercise your vocal cords. But make sure the neighbour's cat or budgie won't join in – it'll be painful enough without accompaniment!

Before the party, prepare song cards, with several well-known songs on each one. Divide all your guests into two teams. Now the first person has to roll the dice. The number on the dice assigns them their "musical instrument" as follows:

1. GUITAR: deng-deng-deng-deng
2. DRUMS: boom-boom-boom
3. FLUTE: wee-wee-wee
4. BANJO: plim-plim-plim
5. COMB: Mmmmm (lips pressed together)
6. SAXOPHONE: mwah-mwah-mwaaah-mwahwah.

Make up alternative instruments if you prefer.

Now the "musician" has to take a song card, and start to "play" the first song on the card. Members of their own team have to guess the tune as quickly as possible, so they can move on to the next song. If the team cannot make head or tail of what they hear, the other team will have a chance to guess.

The same player carries on until their card is finished, then play moves to the other team. Each correctly guessed tune counts as a point; each wrong guess is a point deducted.

Here are some ideas for songs: *Mrs Robinson (Simon & Garfunkel); Roxanne (Police); Theme from the James Bond films; Yesterday (The Beatles); I Was Born Under a Wand'rin' Star (Lee Marvin); Staying Alive (The Bee Gees); What a Wonderful World (Louis Armstrong); Like a Virgin (Madonna); I Will Survive (Gloria Gaynor); You're the One that I Want (Olivia Newton-John); Stand by Your Man (Tammy Wynette); Simply the Best (Tina Turner); Pretty Woman (Roy Orbison).*

Hide-Away

YOU WILL NEED:
A SMALL NUMBER OF PLAYERS
(PAPER AND PEN)

When there is a lull, after a good meal perhaps, you can get everyone going again with a word game that involves a lot of shouting, such as this one.

First, choose a category. This could really be anything, such as modes of transport, types of housing or items of clothing. Now the first player has to pick a word from that category, for example "car", "hut" or "bra", to fit our three sample categories.

Now players take turns in calling out ever longer words that include the chosen word. In our case for example, they could shout "scare", "carpet", "cardiology" which all include "car";

"shutter" which includes "hut"; or "zebra" or "brazier" if the chosen word was "bra".

Players are eliminated if their minds go blank or if they take too long to come up with a reasonable answer – and this game is best played at great speed. You might want to use a time limit, say five seconds for each answer, to increase urgency.

You could play this game in writing, too, if you don't want to wake the neighbours or the children! This will only get noisy once you start comparing results.

Foreign Creatures

YOU WILL NEED:
ANY NUMBER OF GUESTS
PAPER AND PENS

This is really a puzzle, but it's great fun to play on your guests, because it works almost every time and it'll amaze everyone.

Give your guests paper and pen. Now ask them all to think of a number between 1 and 10, and to write it down. Next they should multiply this number by 9, add both digits together, and then subtract 5 from this number.

Play this game quickly, and don't give people too much time to think of extra-clever answers. Now ask your guests to find the letter in the alphabet that is equivalent to their number, if A=1, B=2, C=3, and so on. Once they have their letter, get them to think of a country that begins with it.

Now everyone needs to take the second letter of that

country's name, and think of an animal beginning with that letter.

Lastly, ask everyone to think of a colour. Everyone should now write down the result, reading as "a Colour – an Animal – from a Country". Then guests should turn their papers over.

Surprise your guests – tell them that you are certain you can guess what at least one of them has written down. Close your eyes for better concentration, and let your hands hover above each sheet of paper so that you can feel the vibes emanating from their writing. Finally open your eyes and declare full of conviction: "a grey elephant from Denmark" – try it, you're bound to be right!

Stickety Wickety

YOU WILL NEED:
SIX OR MORE PLAYERS
PAPER AND PENS
TIMER

This is another quick-fire word game played in three stages – you will need your wits about you to pass onto the final level!

Divide your guests into two teams. Give each team paper and pen, then allow them a little time to prepare. Now set the timer to one minute. One team starts by giving a definition, which the other team has to "translate" into Stick Wicks – two rhyming, single-syllable words, for example "a self-satisfied invertebrate" is a "smug slug". They are allowed to continue as long as they guess correctly in the given time. Play passes to the other team, as soon as an incorrect answer is given or time has run out.

Teams can opt to stay on level 1 or move up to the next level, if they feel confident.

On level 2, everything is a little more long-winded, for the answers should be Sticky Wickies – two rhyming two-syllable words. "A long-eared rodent in a happy disposition", for example, translates as a "sunny bunny".

And on level 3 – yes, you got it – the answers are Stickety Wicketies, two rhyming three or more - syllable words, for example, "giving birth in southern Germany by means of surgery" is a "Bavarian Caesarean".

Each team collects 1 point for a correct Stick Wick, 2 for a Sticky Wicky and 3 for a Stickety Wickety. The team with the most points is the winner.

Horse Race

YOU WILL NEED:
TWO TO TEN PLAYERS
2 PACKS OF CARDS
MONEY OR TOKENS

Money makes the world go round – as you will find out in this easy betting game!

Cut for deal. The dealer removes all four Aces from one pack, and places them face up on the table, as if they were horses on the starting line.

Now he takes the second pack, and deals six cards, face down, in a line, at right angles to the starting line. These mark the length of the racecourse and the finish line. The rest of this pack is not needed. The race is ready to commence!

The dealer deals six cards from the first pack, face up, and allocates each of them to the Ace of the same suit, as in the example over the page.

FINISH LINE

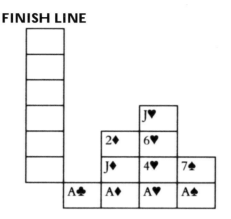

			J♥	
		2♦	6♥	
		J♦	4♥	7♠
	A♣	A♦	A♥	A♠

The dealer now has to give the odds on any suit that players wish to bet on. In this example, Clubs are favourites, as there are twelve cards left in the pack, while Hearts are outsiders. Odds could be evens for Clubs, 2–1 for Diamonds, 3–1 Hearts and 3–2 for Spades.

Now everyone can make their bets, and the dealer starts dealing cards from the pack, face up, moving the appropriate ace forward one space for every card of that suit turned over.

The first ace to travel all six spaces and cross the finish line is the winner. The dealer pays the winners at the agreed odds, and keeps all other tokens. Deal passes to the left.

Candlelight Slander

YOU WILL NEED:
FOUR OR MORE PLAYERS, WITH A
STREAK OF MALICE

Here's your chance to be really nasty to someone else! And that's something we all enjoy from time to time, don't we?

Divide everyone into two teams. Now the teams have to choose a set of public figures, say four famous personalities from TV cookery programmes, football, international politics, and film. Alternatively, you could limit yourselves to just one such category at a time.

Now each team starts to slander and abuse their chosen few. This is best – but more difficult as you cannot mention the name – if it has to be done in the style of some of the racier newspaper headlines. Meanwhile, the other team have to try and guess, as quickly as they can, who is being maligned. You can make up completely unsubstantiated, wild and wicked accusations as you go along, but these will obviously need to stay within the realm of the possible – otherwise your opponents will never guess who you're talking about!

Make sure you use some well-loved figures, too, not only those everyone loves to hate. This makes it a lot more difficult to think of the correct answer, and a lot more fun, too.

But, a word of warning: avoid slandering the other party guests – it's not a pretty sight if an angry wife starts to lay into her husband for never helping with the household chores or for ogling other females. And it will all end in tears if one of the guests uses the opportunity to get all their feelings about host and hostess off their chest!

Some examples for eminently slanderable personalities: *Monica Lewinsky, Roseanne, Tom Cruise, Ken Hom, Liz Taylor, George Bush, Hugh Grant, Mary Poppins, Michael Jackson, Homer Simpson, Scary Spice, O.J. Simpson, Kate Winslet, Donald Duck, Winnie the Pooh.*

Buster Keaton

YOU WILL NEED:
SIX PLAYERS OR MORE
A STRAIGHT FACE

Sometimes, the simplest things just get funnier and funnier – especially, when you're not allowed to laugh or even pull a face!

Everyone sits around in a circle, and one player starts by saying a word or a phrase, or by performing an action. Everyone else in turn has to repeat this, until the action gets back to the first player. All players need to keep a straight face at all times – no laughing, no giggling, no snorting, no knowing grins! Now the next person continues with a new phrase or action, and with the same po-faced expression.

Choose imaginative phrases, or rude words, or tongue-twisters; try pulling silly faces, or doing something to the person next to you. But you'll be

amazed how funny the most trivial

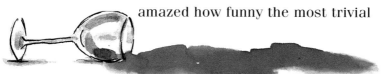

sentences, simple descriptions, or even single words will seem after you've had a few drinks and played this game for a while.

You could describe what you had for breakfast, for example, but make it sound as if it was the most amazing and unusual, yes even daring, thing to have a bowl of cornflakes with milk or a glass of orange juice in the morning! Or you could describe your cat or dog ...

Scoring. All players have three lives, and they lose one every time they burst into uncontrollable giggles or loud howls of laughter. After three lapses, they're out. The last person left is Buster Keaton, the one with the ultimate poker-face – and should really be asked to perform a forfeit for being so utterly straight-laced and humourless!

FOR FORFEIT IDEAS SEE PAGES 18, 42, 60 AND 92

Bottled Knee

YOU WILL NEED:
EIGHT PLAYERS OR MORE
STRING OR MASKING TAPE
TWO EMPTY BOTTLES OR CANS

A physically challenging race, even for the most athletic and sober of your guests.

Divide players into two teams. Create a space in your room and remove all breakable objects. At opposite sides of the room, mark out two lines, using string, chalk or masking tape. Now place two empty bottles on the floor, both behind one of the lines. Plastic bottles are safest for this game.

The object of this relay race is for each member of the team to pick up the bottle and carry it to the opposite line, holding it between their knees or thighs, without using their hands to help.

On the starting signal, the first member of each team tries to pick up the bottle with their knees or

thighs. They are

allowed to

use their mouths at this stage, but not their hands, to help get the bottle in position.

As soon as the bottle is firmly clamped in position, they have to waddle to the other side of the room, as fast as they can – without dropping the bottle and without using their hands to push it back into position – where the next member of the team is waiting to take over.

If a bottle is dropped, the weak-kneed person has to take it back behind their starting line, pick the bottle up, and set off again from there.

Team members are allowed to help each other – if a bottle seems to be slipping out from between exhausted thighs, another member of the same team can come and reposition it, but again they are only allowed to use their mouths or knees, not their hands. (Have a camera ready for some of the more interesting activities here!)

The winner is the first team to have completed the "bottled knee" course – and a *full* bottle should be ready and waiting because, after all their hard work, they'll definitely need a drink!

How do you like it?

YOU WILL NEED:
ANY NUMBER OF GUESTS,
WHO ARE INTO 'DOUBLE ENTENDRES'

Innuendo is the name of this guessing game. You'll be surprised how many people enjoy being just a little bit saucy!

One player leaves the room, while the others think of an object or a pastime. This should preferably be as innocent and everyday as possible. The player then has to come back in and guess what it is, by addressing each person in turn with the  same three questions: "How do you like it?" – "When do you like it?" – and "Where do you like it?"

The fun of the game lies in keeping a straight face while coming up with suggestive responses. The game is best played very fast.

Some ideas for what you could choose: *A Boiled Egg, Chocolate Cake, Diet Cola, Knitting, A Game of American Football, An Argument, Sunbathing, A Dressing Down by the Boss, A Vacation, Driving, A Hamburger, A Pay Rise, A Flower* – anything really, but the more trivial and non-sexy, the better!

And here's how the dialogue might develop:

"How do you like it?"

Player 1: "hard";

Player 2: "soft";

Player 3: "a bit like this, and a bit like that".

"When do you like it?"

Player 1: "first thing in the morning";

Player 2: "at most once a week";

Player 3: "as often as I can get it".

"Where do you like it?"

Player 1: "in the kitchen";

Player 2: "on the table";

Player 3: "in my mouth". … Well!

Debating Club

YOU WILL NEED:
ABOUT SIX TO TEN PLAYERS
PEN AND PAPER

Are your friends argumentative? Give them something to get their teeth into!

Divide all players into two teams, ideally in separate rooms. Give each team pen and paper, and about five minutes to think up and write down some completely obvious, true, sensible and reasonable statements.

Alternatively, prepare your own statements in advance. This would allow you to tailor the statements to the particular guests you have invited.

When the teams

 reconvene, they should take it in turn to present a statement to a specific opponent. Their opponents will have to argue vehemently and passionately against this statement, whether or not they would normally agree.

This game gets funnier, the more a statement is tailored to a specific person. If, for example, one guest is a die-hard sexist, you could give him a provocative statement about women's rights; a smoker might have to persuade others of the dangers of smoking; or, something altogether more mundane, ask your opponent to prove that a Monday is not a Monday, and that a table is not a table!

At the end, each team has to judge their opponents' efforts and give them marks out of five for persuasiveness and conviction.

One word of caution: many statements will revolve around beliefs and convictions, be they of a political, moral or religious nature. Not everyone takes such fundamental beliefs lightly, and you might upset your guests if you are not careful!

Drink a Tower

YOU WILL NEED:
A SMALL ROUND OF THIRSTY GUESTS
TWO DICE
A NUMBER OF BEER MATS OR SIMILAR
SMALLER AND LARGER GLASSES WITH BEERS AND CHASERS

This is a drinking game, only suited for those well versed in downing a few.

Throw the dice and follow these rules:

- two different numbers = build the tower: in sequence, place first a full beer glass, then a beer mat on top, next a chaser on the beer mat, then another beer and so on. Build a second tower if the first one is beginning to look wobbly;

- two numbers the same = drink the most recent set, i.e. one beer, one chaser;

- one and six = drink the entire tower(s).

Carry on playing for as long as you and your guests wish or are able to without toppling over…!

Forfeits

AND ANOTHER TEN IDEAS FOR FORFEITS

1. In less than two minutes, make up a limerick about your host or hostess.

2. Kiss the left ear of everyone who's playing.

3. Imitate a baboon for 3 minutes.

4. Remove an item of underwear, in view of everyone, without leaving the room.

5. Crawl out of the room on your stomach or do ten press-ups.

6. Sing a song that mentions at least one garden vegetable or one mode of transport.

7. Persuade or bribe someone in the room to allow you to hit them.

8. Don't touch your own drink for 10 minutes.

9. Finish the drink on your left.

10. Do an Elvis Presley impression.

In Tune

YOU WILL NEED:
A SMALL GROUP OF PLAYERS
PAPER AND PEN FOR EACH PERSON
2 BOWLS OR HATS
AN EGG TIMER

This is a variation of the all-time favourite After Dinner Game, Scattergories.

If organized, it's best to prepare in advance for this game by cutting up lots of bits of paper (about the size of a credit card). On half of these bits of paper, you or your guests write a different letter of the alphabet, then fold them in two and put them in a bowl. On the other half you write different categories, such as perfume brands or items of clothing (for more category ideas see the next page).

Equip each player with pen and paper. Then one

player (the winner from another game) can choose six letters and six categories. The player reads them out to the other players, who in turn should write the letters down the left-hand side of the paper and the categories across the top.

Set the timer. As quickly as possible, players have to fill in their grid, finding an entry for each category that starts with each of the six letters. The game stops when the time has run out or when the first player has filled in their grid.

Now everyone reads out their words. Points are awarded if a player has managed to guess what the other players will write down. So, if several players think of "New York" as a city starting with "N", they may award themselves 1 point each. If, however, they are the only one with that answer and everyone else has written New Orleans, they have to deduct 5 points from their score.

Ideas for categories: *Countries, Flowers, Boys' Names, Pizza Toppings, Terms of Endearment, Cars Driven By TV Heroes and Heroines, Salad Dressings, Holiday Resorts, Swear Words.*

Last Laughs

YOU WILL NEED:
EIGHT PLAYERS OR MORE
NAME CARDS FOR ALL THOSE PRESENT
TWO BOXES
PENS

This game is quite evil, but – let's face it – some people need to be taught a lesson!

In advance, write the names of all those who were invited on a card. Before guests arrive, place their name cards into two boxes, keeping men's and women's names separate.

When all guests are present, get every woman to pick a name from the men's box, and every man to pick one from the women's box. Issue your guests with pens, and ask them to think of a forfeit and write it on their cards – something that should be performed, done,

**FOR
FORFEIT
IDEAS
SEE PAGES
18, 42, 60
AND 92**

exhibited, answered, sung, rhymed, kissed, promised, confessed...

But – and herein lies the shock – instead of passing the cards to the named person, as might have been expected, and asking them to do the forfeit that had been devised especially for them, the host or hostess will now ask every guest to read out their own forfeit and perform it!

This will bring an instant shock, and much cause for merriment later, when the forfeits are being performed, as people inevitably come up with some very silly commands.

Results are particularly hilarious, because they were often – mistakenly – aimed at the opposite sex, for example "X should give me all his money" – in which case reverse the action; "Y should snog the host for three minutes" – this might be aimed at a man; or "Z should strip and run once around the table" – the writer will have to do it him- or herself!

It is now obvious why the game is sometimes also called "Do-As-You-Would-Be-Done-By" ...

Hangman

YOU WILL NEED:
SIX TO TEN PLAYERS
ONE HANGMAN
A PIECE OF STRING

You can test everyone's powers of reaction with this game – not a bad idea if they are preparing to drive home!

Ask everyone to sit around a small table, and choose a hangman. The hangman could dress up with a black hood, and you could dim the lights, to add to the sinister atmosphere.

All players now reach forward and press the index finger of one hand upright against everyone else's index fingers, in a circle in the centre of the table.

The hangman makes a running noose out of the piece of string, and slips this over the grouped finger tips, while holding onto the end of the string. The hangman slowly walks around the table, and probably mumbles some medieval Latin prayers. Suddenly, though, they will shout "Death!", and quickly jerk up the string. Players have to whip their fingers away, because if their reflexes are slow, their fingers will be executed. They will either be out of the game – and have to perform a forfeit – or they'll have to take over from the hangman.

And, of course, if they get caught, they really shouldn't drive home!

Quack Quack

YOU WILL NEED:
ANY NUMBER OF PLAYERS, THE MORE
THE NOISIER

This game will give your guests the ideal chance to let their hair down and, for once, be really, really quackers!

So, once dinner's been eaten, the plates have been cleared and coffee's been served, one player has to leave the room. Now everyone else decides on an action that they will have to perform as they come back in. This could, of course, be anything – the more ridiculous, the better: scratching their head; taking their shoes off; snogging a particular person; laughing hysterically; hopping around on one leg; taking a drink from the table and finishing it in one; or even stripping down to the waist.

As the player comes back in, they have to guess what they are meant to do. The other players help, but without saying anything. Instead they have to quack continuously and quietly, all the time.

As soon as the player gets "warmer", that is closer to performing what is required of them, the quacking should get louder and faster, showing them that they are on the right track.

Similarly, if the player starts moving away again, in the wrong direction, or begins to perform something that is further removed from the intended activity, the quacking has to die down again.

Once the player has guessed correctly – and performed the feat that has been demanded of them – it is the next person's turn. But remember: if you came up with a particularly ridiculous action, it could be your turn next!

To ring the changes, you could change the animal noises, too; monkeys, pigs, cows and frogs are all equally entertaining guides.

Inebriated Newts

YOU WILL NEED:
EIGHT PLAYERS OR MORE
PREPARED NEWT CARDS

A memory game, perfectly suited to the fag-end of a long night's drinking!

Prepare your "newt" cards in advance. Each card should have a number, from 1 to 16, and feature an inane phrase including that number, preferably using alliteration, or being difficult to pronounce.

Now the first player has to pick a card, and read it aloud, without showing it to the others. Everyone else, going around in a circle, repeats. Player 1 then takes a second card, and says what was written on both cards, without referring back. Everybody else repeats. This continues until Player

FOR
FORFEIT
IDEAS
SEE PAGES
18, 42, 60
AND 92

1 finishes all the cards. Now it starts again, with the player to the left!

If anyone forgets one of the phrases, gets them wrong, or just stutters unfathomable rubbish, they'll probably need another drink. Here are some extremely silly examples for you to better:

1. One hand; One band; One grand
2. A couple of trucks; A couple of bucks
3. Three steep stairs; Three brown bears
4. Four town squares; Four second-hand chairs
5. Five pairs of Mrs Zoomer's Bloomers
6. Six thousand rushing Micronesians in full battle array; Six typewritten letters on a sleigh
7. Seven seasoned sizzling sausages in the pan
8. Eight eldest sons; Eight old buns; Eight Huns
9. Nine tons of wasted skate; Nine carts of bait
10. Ten tired tortoises tripping tiredly to Thailand
11. Eleven male whales; Eleven eager beavers
12. 12 bells of Hell; 12 combs in tortoise-shell
13. 13 thousand rusty nails in pails with snails
14. 14 swaying palms on a balmy tropical shore
15. 15 letching lecturers learning the lessons of love

Reservoir Snogs

YOU WILL NEED:
EIGHT GUESTS OR MORE
A BLINDFOLD

A "friendly" way to say good-bye, after a lovely meal, at the end of a delightful evening, with old and new friends…

Blindfold one player, then ask the others to form a circle around them. Turn the blindfolded player until they're a little dizzy, and won't know who's where.

Next they have to stumble towards one of the players, kiss them with maximum enthusiasm full on the mouth – and guess who they've kissed! As they now know everyone who's present, they stand a good chance of getting it right, or do they? If they get it right, they can swap places with that person, if not, they'll just have to try again!

A word of warning: beware the amorous letch that repeatedly gets it wrong!

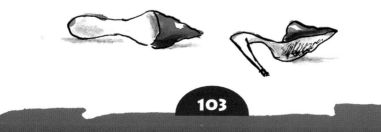

Other titles published by Lagoon Books

GAMES BOOKS

50 of the Finest Drinking Games ISBN 1899712178
50 of the Finest Adult Party Games ISBN 1902813065

BOTTLE BOOKS

Lateral Thinking Puzzles ISBN 1899712208
Trivia Quiz ISBN 1899712216
Pub Joke Book ISBN 1899712224

All books can be ordered from bookshops by quoting the above ISBN numbers.

For more titles, visit Lagoon Books' website
www.lagoongames.com